# THIS

# TOURING

# WITH A

# MOTORHOME

# TRAVEL JOURNAL

## BELONGS TO

NAME ....ANDY & LYNDA....................................

EMAIL ....LYNDAJOS@outlook.com...............

MOBILE ....07702666331..............................

BLOG ...........................................................

## PLEASE RETURN IF FOUND

# MOTORHOME
# TRAVEL JOURNAL

DATE ...15.5.2023...    MILEAGE START ........................

START TIME ...............    MILEAGE END ........................

ARRIVAL TIME ...............    MILEAGE TOTAL ........................

---

CAMPSITE NAME ...LITTLE NORTH LEIGH FARM.......

ADDRESS 1 ........................................................

ADDRESS 2 ........................................................

POST CODE .....................    GPS ...............................

E MAIL ...........................    PHONE ...........................

WEBSITE WWW ...............................................

MY RATING ☆ ☆ ☆ ☆ ☆    NUMBER OF NIGHTS HERE ..2..

WEATHER ...........................    TEMPERATURE .....................

---

## WILDCAMPING LOCATION NOTES

........................................................................

........................................................................

........................................................................

........................................................................

.............................. GPS ...................................

---

| DAILY COSTS | TODAY'S HIGHLIGHTS |
|---|---|
| SITE FEES pn. £ 15-00 | ................................ |
| FUEL £ ..................... | ................................ |
| PROPANE £ ..................... | ................................ |
| TOLLS £ ..................... | ................................ |
| GROCERIES £ ..................... | ................................ |
| DINING OUT £ ..................... | ................................ |
| ENTERTAINMENT £ ..................... | ................................ |
| OTHER COSTS £ ..................... | ................................ |

## TO DO TOMORROW

........................................................................

........................................................................

........................................................................

........................................................................

# NOTES

........................................................................................................

........................................................................................................

........................................................................................................

........................................................................................................

........................................................................................................

........................................................................................................

........................................................................................................

........................................................................................................

# SKETCH / KEEPSAKE / PHOTOGRAPH

# MOTORHOME
# TRAVEL JOURNAL

DATE .17.5.2023... MILEAGE START 4429......

START TIME ...6am.. MILEAGE END 4703.......

ARRIVAL TIME ................ MILEAGE TOTAL ......................

---

CAMPSITE NAME ..LITTLE SATMAR................................

ADDRESS 1 ........................................................

ADDRESS 2 ........................................................

POST CODE ..................... GPS ................................

E MAIL ........................... PHONE .............................

WEBSITE WWW ....................................................

MY RATING ☆  ☆  ☆  ☆  ☆  NUMBER OF NIGHTS HERE ......

WEATHER ........................... TEMPERATURE ......................

---

## WILDCAMPING LOCATION NOTES

................................................................
................................................................
................................................................
................................................................
......................................... GPS ........................

---

| DAILY COSTS | | TODAY'S HIGHLIGHTS |
|---|---|---|
| SITE FEES | £ ..................... | .................................. |
| FUEL | £ ..................... | .................................. |
| PROPANE | £ ..................... | .................................. |
| TOLLS | £ ..................... | .................................. |
| GROCERIES | £ ..................... | .................................. |
| DINING OUT | £ ..................... | .................................. |
| ENTERTAINMENT | £ ..................... | .................................. |
| OTHER COSTS | £ ..................... | .................................. |

## TO DO TOMORROW

................................................................
................................................................
................................................................
................................................................

# NOTES

........................................................................

........................................................................

........................................................................

........................................................................

........................................................................

........................................................................

........................................................................

## SKETCH / KEEPSAKE / PHOTOGRAPH

# MOTORHOME
# TRAVEL JOURNAL

DATE ..18.5..2023. MILEAGE START .........................

START TIME ................ MILEAGE END .........................

ARRIVAL TIME ................ MILEAGE TOTAL .........................

CAMPSITE NAME .....~~LITTLE SAJMAR~~.. KNAUS............

ADDRESS 1 ...................................................................

ADDRESS 2 ...................................................................

POST CODE ..................... GPS ...............................

E MAIL ......................... PHONE ...............................

WEBSITE WWW ...............................................................

MY RATING ☆ ☆ ☆ ☆ ☆ NUMBER OF NIGHTS HERE ..2.

WEATHER .......................... TEMPERATURE .........................

## WILDCAMPING LOCATION NOTES

..................................................................................
..................................................................................
..................................................................................
..................................................................................
........................................ GPS ...............................

| DAILY COSTS | | TODAY'S HIGHLIGHTS |
|---|---|---|
| SITE FEES | £ ................ | ................................ |
| FUEL | £ ................ | ................................ |
| PROPANE | £ ................ | ................................ |
| TOLLS | £ ................ | ................................ |
| GROCERIES | £ ................ | ................................ |
| DINING OUT | £ ................ | ................................ |
| ENTERTAINMENT | £ ................ | ................................ |
| OTHER COSTS | £ ................ | ................................ |

## TO DO TOMORROW

..................................................................................
..................................................................................
..................................................................................
..................................................................................

# NOTES

.............................................................................................................

.............................................................................................................

.............................................................................................................

.............................................................................................................

.............................................................................................................

.............................................................................................................

.............................................................................................................

.............................................................................................................

## SKETCH / KEEPSAKE / PHOTOGRAPH

# MOTORHOME
# TRAVEL JOURNAL

DATE ..20.5.2023.. MILEAGE START .........................

START TIME ................ MILEAGE END .........................

ARRIVAL TIME ................ MILEAGE TOTAL .........................

---

CAMPSITE NAME ..HANSE CAMPING.........................

ADDRESS 1 .........................

ADDRESS 2 .........................

POST CODE ..................... GPS .........................

E MAIL ......................... PHONE .........................

WEBSITE WWW .........................

MY RATING ☆ ☆ ☆ ☆ ☆ NUMBER OF NIGHTS HERE ..2..

WEATHER ......................... TEMPERATURE .........................

---

## WILDCAMPING LOCATION NOTES

...............................................................

...............................................................

...............................................................

...............................................................

............................... GPS ...............................

---

## DAILY COSTS

SITE FEES £ .....................

FUEL £ .....................

PROPANE £ .....................

TOLLS £ .....................

GROCERIES £ .....................

DINING OUT £ .....................

ENTERTAINMENT £ .....................

OTHER COSTS £ .....................

## TODAY'S HIGHLIGHTS

...............................

...............................

...............................

...............................

...............................

...............................

...............................

## TO DO TOMORROW

...............................................................

...............................................................

...............................................................

...............................................................

# NOTES

........................................................................................................

........................................................................................................

........................................................................................................

........................................................................................................

........................................................................................................

........................................................................................................

........................................................................................................

........................................................................................................

## SKETCH / KEEPSAKE / PHOTOGRAPH

# MOTORHOME TRAVEL JOURNAL

DATE .22..5..2023. MILEAGE START ........................

START TIME ................. MILEAGE END ........................

ARRIVAL TIME ................. MILEAGE TOTAL ........................

CAMPSITE NAME .RIBE CAMPING..............................

ADDRESS 1 ..................................................

ADDRESS 2 ..................................................

POST CODE ..................... GPS ........................

E MAIL ........................... PHONE ........................

WEBSITE WWW ..................................................

MY RATING ☆ ☆ ☆ ☆ ☆ NUMBER OF NIGHTS HERE ..2.

WEATHER ........................... TEMPERATURE ........................

## WILDCAMPING LOCATION NOTES

..................................................
..................................................
..................................................
..................................................
.............................. GPS ........................

## DAILY COSTS

| | | TODAY'S HIGHLIGHTS |
|---|---|---|
| SITE FEES | £ ................ | ........................ |
| FUEL | £ ................ | ........................ |
| PROPANE | £ ................ | ........................ |
| TOLLS | £ ................ | ........................ |
| GROCERIES | £ ................ | ........................ |
| DINING OUT | £ ................ | ........................ |
| ENTERTAINMENT | £ ................ | ........................ |
| OTHER COSTS | £ ................ | ........................ |

## TO DO TOMORROW

..................................................
..................................................
..................................................
..................................................

# NOTES

.........................................................................................................

.........................................................................................................

.........................................................................................................

.........................................................................................................

.........................................................................................................

.........................................................................................................

.........................................................................................................

.........................................................................................................

## SKETCH / KEEPSAKE / PHOTOGRAPH

# MOTORHOME
# TRAVEL JOURNAL

DATE _24. 5. 2023_  MILEAGE START ........................

START TIME ................  MILEAGE END .........................

ARRIVAL TIME ................  MILEAGE TOTAL .........................

CAMPSITE NAME _Kristiansand Feriesenter._ ..............

ADDRESS 1 ............................................................

ADDRESS 2 ............................................................

POST CODE ...................... GPS ...................................

E MAIL ........................... PHONE ..............................

WEBSITE WWW ............................................................

MY RATING ☆ ☆ ☆ ☆ ☆  NUMBER OF NIGHTS HERE .._1_...

WEATHER ........................... TEMPERATURE .........................

## WILDCAMPING LOCATION NOTES

........................................................................
........................................................................
........................................................................
........................................................................
........................... GPS ...................................

| DAILY COSTS | | TODAY'S HIGHLIGHTS |
|---|---|---|
| SITE FEES | £ ................ | ........................... |
| FUEL | £ ................ | ........................... |
| PROPANE | £ ................ | ........................... |
| TOLLS | £ ................ | ........................... |
| GROCERIES | £ ................ | ........................... |
| DINING OUT | £ ................ | ........................... |
| ENTERTAINMENT | £ ................ | ........................... |
| OTHER COSTS | £ ................ | ........................... |

## TO DO TOMORROW

........................................................................
........................................................................
........................................................................
........................................................................

# NOTES

.................................................................................................................

.................................................................................................................

.................................................................................................................

.................................................................................................................

.................................................................................................................

.................................................................................................................

.................................................................................................................

.................................................................................................................

## SKETCH / KEEPSAKE / PHOTOGRAPH

# MOTORHOME
# TRAVEL JOURNAL

DATE .25.5.2023 MILEAGE START 5321..........

START TIME 9.16 am MILEAGE END ...................

ARRIVAL TIME 14.30 pm MILEAGE TOTAL ...................

CAMPSITE NAME Camping Preikestolen..........

ADDRESS 1 ...................................................

ADDRESS 2 ...................................................

POST CODE ................... GPS ..............................

E MAIL ........................ PHONE ..............................

WEBSITE WWW ...................................................

MY RATING ☆ ☆ ☆ ☆ ☆ NUMBER OF NIGHTS HERE 2..

WEATHER ......................... TEMPERATURE ...................

## WILDCAMPING LOCATION NOTES

................................................................
................................................................
................................................................
................................................................
................................. GPS ..........................

| DAILY COSTS | | TODAY'S HIGHLIGHTS |
|---|---|---|
| SITE FEES | £ ................ | ............................... |
| FUEL | £ ................ | ............................... |
| PROPANE | £ ................ | ............................... |
| TOLLS | £ ................ | ............................... |
| GROCERIES | £ ................ | ............................... |
| DINING OUT | £ ................ | ............................... |
| ENTERTAINMENT | £ ................ | ............................... |
| OTHER COSTS | £ ................ | ............................... |

## TO DO TOMORROW

................................................................
................................................................
................................................................
................................................................

# NOTES

Got a bit lost! Added 1½hrs to
journey. Stopped by a fjord
for a break.
Passed through Ryfylke Tunnel
- longest road tunnel
undersea in the world.

## SKETCH / KEEPSAKE / PHOTOGRAPH

# MOTORHOME
# TRAVEL JOURNAL

DATE .....27. 5. 2023...... MILEAGE START ........................

START TIME ............... MILEAGE END ........................

ARRIVAL TIME ............... MILEAGE TOTAL ........................

---

CAMPSITE NAME Eikhamrane Camping.............

ADDRESS I ...........................................

ADDRESS 2 ...........................................

POST CODE .................... GPS ...........................

E MAIL ........................ PHONE ...........................

WEBSITE WWW ...........................................

MY RATING ☆ ☆ ☆ ☆ ☆ NUMBER OF NIGHTS HERE ..2..

WEATHER ....................... TEMPERATURE .......................

---

## WILDCAMPING LOCATION NOTES

...........................................
...........................................
...........................................
...........................................
.......................... GPS .......................

---

| DAILY COSTS | | TODAY'S HIGHLIGHTS |
|---|---|---|
| SITE FEES | £ ..................... | ........................... |
| FUEL | £ ..................... | ........................... |
| PROPANE | £ ..................... | ........................... |
| TOLLS | £ ..................... | ........................... |
| GROCERIES | £ ..................... | ........................... |
| DINING OUT | £ ..................... | ........................... |
| ENTERTAINMENT | £ ..................... | ........................... |
| OTHER COSTS | £ ..................... | ........................... |

## TO DO TOMORROW

...........................................

...........................................

...........................................

...........................................

# NOTES

Camping directly onto
Hardangerfjord – stunning
Visit to cider Farm – ate
cured lamb & ham & tasted
4 different ciders

## SKETCH / KEEPSAKE / PHOTOGRAPH

# MOTORHOME
# TRAVEL JOURNAL

DATE  29.5.2023          MILEAGE START ......................
START TIME  ...............  MILEAGE END  ......................
ARRIVAL TIME  ...............  MILEAGE TOTAL ......................

CAMPSITE NAME  Flåm Camping ......................
ADDRESS 1 ......................................................
ADDRESS 2 ......................................................
POST CODE ....................  GPS ..............................
E MAIL ...........................  PHONE ..........................
WEBSITE WWW ..................................................
MY RATING ☆ ☆ ☆ ☆ ☆   NUMBER OF NIGHTS HERE  3
WEATHER ..........................  TEMPERATURE ......................

## WILDCAMPING LOCATION NOTES

................................................................
................................................................
................................................................
................................................................
................................ GPS ..............................

## DAILY COSTS              ## TODAY'S HIGHLIGHTS

SITE FEES       £ ....................   ......................
FUEL            £ ....................   ......................
PROPANE         £ ....................   ......................
TOLLS           £ ....................   ......................
GROCERIES       £ ....................   ......................
DINING OUT      £ ....................   ......................
ENTERTAINMENT   £ ....................   ......................
OTHER COSTS     £ ....................   ......................

## TO DO TOMORROW

................................................................
................................................................
................................................................
................................................................

# NOTES

........................................................................................................

........................................................................................................

........................................................................................................

........................................................................................................

........................................................................................................

........................................................................................................

........................................................................................................

........................................................................................................

## SKETCH / KEEPSAKE / PHOTOGRAPH

# MOTORHOME
# TRAVEL JOURNAL

DATE ..................... MILEAGE START .........................

START TIME ................ MILEAGE END .........................

ARRIVAL TIME ............... MILEAGE TOTAL .........................

CAMPSITE NAME ..............................................

ADDRESS I ..................................................

ADDRESS 2 ..................................................

POST CODE ..................... GPS ..........................

E MAIL ......................... PHONE .......................

WEBSITE WWW ................................................

MY RATING ☆ ☆ ☆ ☆ ☆ NUMBER OF NIGHTS HERE ......

WEATHER ......................... TEMPERATURE .................

## WILDCAMPING LOCATION NOTES

.............................................................
.............................................................
.............................................................
.............................................................
.................................... GPS ....................

## DAILY COSTS

| | | |
|---|---|---|
| SITE FEES | £ | ..................... |
| FUEL | £ | ..................... |
| PROPANE | £ | ..................... |
| TOLLS | £ | ..................... |
| GROCERIES | £ | ..................... |
| DINING OUT | £ | ..................... |
| ENTERTAINMENT | £ | ..................... |
| OTHER COSTS | £ | ..................... |

## TODAY'S HIGHLIGHTS

.............................................
.............................................
.............................................
.............................................
.............................................
.............................................
.............................................

## TO DO TOMORROW

.............................................................
.............................................................
.............................................................
.............................................................

# NOTES

........................................................................................................

........................................................................................................

........................................................................................................

........................................................................................................

........................................................................................................

........................................................................................................

........................................................................................................

........................................................................................................

## SKETCH / KEEPSAKE / PHOTOGRAPH

# MOTORHOME
# TRAVEL JOURNAL

DATE ..................... MILEAGE START ........................

START TIME ............... MILEAGE END ........................

ARRIVAL TIME ............... MILEAGE TOTAL ........................

---

CAMPSITE NAME ..........................................

ADDRESS 1 ..............................................

ADDRESS 2 ..............................................

POST CODE ................... GPS ......................

E MAIL ...................... PHONE ....................

WEBSITE WWW .........................................

MY RATING ☆ ☆ ☆ ☆ ☆ NUMBER OF NIGHTS HERE ......

WEATHER ......................... TEMPERATURE ...................

---

## WILDCAMPING LOCATION NOTES

..............................................................
..............................................................
..............................................................
..............................................................
............................... GPS ..........................

| DAILY COSTS | TODAY'S HIGHLIGHTS |
|---|---|
| SITE FEES £ ................... | ................... |
| FUEL £ ................... | ................... |
| PROPANE £ ................... | ................... |
| TOLLS £ ................... | ................... |
| GROCERIES £ ................... | ................... |
| DINING OUT £ ................... | ................... |
| ENTERTAINMENT £ ................... | ................... |
| OTHER COSTS £ ................... | ................... |

## TO DO TOMORROW

..............................................................
..............................................................
..............................................................
..............................................................

# NOTES

........................................................................................................................

........................................................................................................................

........................................................................................................................

........................................................................................................................

........................................................................................................................

........................................................................................................................

........................................................................................................................

........................................................................................................................

## SKETCH / KEEPSAKE / PHOTOGRAPH

# MOTORHOME
# TRAVEL JOURNAL

DATE ..................... MILEAGE START .........................

START TIME .............. MILEAGE END .......................

ARRIVAL TIME ............... MILEAGE TOTAL .......................

---

CAMPSITE NAME ............................................................

ADDRESS 1 ...............................................................

ADDRESS 2 ...............................................................

POST CODE ..................... GPS ....................................

E MAIL .......................... PHONE .................................

WEBSITE WWW ........................................................

MY RATING ☆ ☆ ☆ ☆ ☆ NUMBER OF NIGHTS HERE ......

WEATHER .......................... TEMPERATURE .......................

---

## WILDCAMPING LOCATION NOTES

...........................................................................
...........................................................................
...........................................................................
...........................................................................
.................................... GPS ...................................

---

| DAILY COSTS | | TODAY'S HIGHLIGHTS |
|---|---|---|
| SITE FEES | £ ..................... | ................................ |
| FUEL | £ ..................... | ................................ |
| PROPANE | £ ..................... | ................................ |
| TOLLS | £ ..................... | ................................ |
| GROCERIES | £ ..................... | ................................ |
| DINING OUT | £ ..................... | ................................ |
| ENTERTAINMENT | £ ..................... | ................................ |
| OTHER COSTS | £ ..................... | ................................ |

## TO DO TOMORROW

...........................................................................
...........................................................................
...........................................................................
...........................................................................

# NOTES

.......................................................................................

.......................................................................................

.......................................................................................

.......................................................................................

.......................................................................................

.......................................................................................

.......................................................................................

## SKETCH / KEEPSAKE / PHOTOGRAPH

# MOTORHOME
# TRAVEL JOURNAL

DATE ..................... MILEAGE START ........................

START TIME ............... MILEAGE END ........................

ARRIVAL TIME ............... MILEAGE TOTAL ........................

---

CAMPSITE NAME ....................................................

ADDRESS 1 ....................................................

ADDRESS 2 ....................................................

POST CODE ..................... GPS ...............................

E MAIL ......................... PHONE ...............................

WEBSITE WWW ....................................................

MY RATING ☆ ☆ ☆ ☆ ☆ NUMBER OF NIGHTS HERE ......

WEATHER .......................... TEMPERATURE .....................

---

## WILDCAMPING LOCATION NOTES

....................................................
....................................................
....................................................
....................................................
............................... GPS .....................

---

| DAILY COSTS | | TODAY'S HIGHLIGHTS |
|---|---|---|
| SITE FEES | £ ..................... | .................................... |
| FUEL | £ ..................... | .................................... |
| PROPANE | £ ..................... | .................................... |
| TOLLS | £ ..................... | .................................... |
| GROCERIES | £ ..................... | .................................... |
| DINING OUT | £ ..................... | .................................... |
| ENTERTAINMENT | £ ..................... | .................................... |
| OTHER COSTS | £ ..................... | .................................... |

## TO DO TOMORROW

....................................................
....................................................
....................................................
....................................................

# NOTES

........................................................................................................

........................................................................................................

........................................................................................................

........................................................................................................

........................................................................................................

........................................................................................................

........................................................................................................

........................................................................................................

## SKETCH / KEEPSAKE / PHOTOGRAPH

# MOTORHOME
# TRAVEL JOURNAL

DATE ...................... MILEAGE START ........................

START TIME ............... MILEAGE END ........................

ARRIVAL TIME ............... MILEAGE TOTAL ........................

---

CAMPSITE NAME ...........................................................

ADDRESS 1 ...............................................................

ADDRESS 2 ...............................................................

POST CODE ..................... GPS ...............................

E MAIL ........................... PHONE ...........................

WEBSITE WWW ...........................................................

MY RATING ☆ ☆ ☆ ☆ ☆ NUMBER OF NIGHTS HERE ......

WEATHER ........................... TEMPERATURE ......................

---

## WILDCAMPING LOCATION NOTES

..................................................................................
..................................................................................
..................................................................................
..................................................................................
............................................ GPS ..............................

---

| DAILY COSTS | | TODAY'S HIGHLIGHTS |
|---|---|---|
| SITE FEES | £ ..................... | ............................... |
| FUEL | £ ..................... | ............................... |
| PROPANE | £ ..................... | ............................... |
| TOLLS | £ ..................... | ............................... |
| GROCERIES | £ ..................... | ............................... |
| DINING OUT | £ ..................... | ............................... |
| ENTERTAINMENT | £ ..................... | ............................... |
| OTHER COSTS | £ ..................... | ............................... |

## TO DO TOMORROW

..................................................................................

..................................................................................

..................................................................................

..................................................................................

# NOTES

........................................................................................

........................................................................................

........................................................................................

........................................................................................

........................................................................................

........................................................................................

........................................................................................

........................................................................................

## SKETCH / KEEPSAKE / PHOTOGRAPH

# MOTORHOME
# TRAVEL JOURNAL

DATE ..................... MILEAGE START .......................

START TIME .............. MILEAGE END .......................

ARRIVAL TIME ............... MILEAGE TOTAL .......................

---

CAMPSITE NAME ........................................

ADDRESS 1 ........................................

ADDRESS 2 ........................................

POST CODE .................... GPS ........................

E MAIL .......................... PHONE ........................

WEBSITE WWW ........................................

MY RATING ☆ ☆ ☆ ☆ ☆ NUMBER OF NIGHTS HERE ......

WEATHER ......................... TEMPERATURE .......................

---

## WILDCAMPING LOCATION NOTES

..............................................................
..............................................................
..............................................................
..............................................................
............................ GPS ...............................

---

| DAILY COSTS | TODAY'S HIGHLIGHTS |
|---|---|
| SITE FEES £ ..................... | ............................ |
| FUEL £ ..................... | ............................ |
| PROPANE £ ..................... | ............................ |
| TOLLS £ ..................... | ............................ |
| GROCERIES £ ..................... | ............................ |
| DINING OUT £ ..................... | ............................ |
| ENTERTAINMENT £ ..................... | ............................ |
| OTHER COSTS £ ..................... | |

## TO DO TOMORROW

..............................................................
..............................................................
..............................................................
..............................................................

# NOTES

.................................................................................................

.................................................................................................

.................................................................................................

.................................................................................................

.................................................................................................

.................................................................................................

.................................................................................................

## SKETCH / KEEPSAKE / PHOTOGRAPH

# MOTORHOME
# TRAVEL JOURNAL

DATE ...................... MILEAGE START ........................

START TIME ................ MILEAGE END ........................

ARRIVAL TIME ................ MILEAGE TOTAL ........................

---

CAMPSITE NAME ..........................................................

ADDRESS 1 ..............................................................

ADDRESS 2 ..............................................................

POST CODE ...................... GPS ..................................

E MAIL ........................... PHONE ................................

WEBSITE WWW ..........................................................

MY RATING ☆ ☆ ☆ ☆ ☆ NUMBER OF NIGHTS HERE ......

WEATHER .......................... TEMPERATURE ......................

---

## WILDCAMPING LOCATION NOTES

......................................................................

......................................................................

......................................................................

......................................................................

.............................. GPS ..................................

| DAILY COSTS | | TODAY'S HIGHLIGHTS |
|---|---|---|
| SITE FEES | £ ............... | ............................ |
| FUEL | £ ............... | ............................ |
| PROPANE | £ ............... | ............................ |
| TOLLS | £ ............... | ............................ |
| GROCERIES | £ ............... | ............................ |
| DINING OUT | £ ............... | ............................ |
| ENTERTAINMENT | £ ............... | ............................ |
| OTHER COSTS | £ ............... | ............................ |

## TO DO TOMORROW

......................................................................

......................................................................

......................................................................

......................................................................

# NOTES

........................................................................................

........................................................................................

........................................................................................

........................................................................................

........................................................................................

........................................................................................

........................................................................................

........................................................................................

## SKETCH / KEEPSAKE / PHOTOGRAPH

# MOTORHOME
# TRAVEL JOURNAL

DATE ..................... MILEAGE START ........................

START TIME ............... MILEAGE END ........................

ARRIVAL TIME ............. MILEAGE TOTAL ........................

---

CAMPSITE NAME ............................................

ADDRESS I ................................................

ADDRESS 2 ................................................

POST CODE .................... GPS ........................

E MAIL ........................ PHONE .....................

WEBSITE WWW ..............................................

MY RATING ☆ ☆ ☆ ☆ ☆ NUMBER OF NIGHTS HERE ......

WEATHER ......................... TEMPERATURE .....................

---

## WILDCAMPING LOCATION NOTES

...............................................................
...............................................................
...............................................................
...............................................................
............................... GPS ..............................

---

| DAILY COSTS | | TODAY'S HIGHLIGHTS |
|---|---|---|
| SITE FEES | £ ................. | ............................... |
| FUEL | £ ................. | ............................... |
| PROPANE | £ ................. | ............................... |
| TOLLS | £ ................. | ............................... |
| GROCERIES | £ ................. | ............................... |
| DINING OUT | £ ................. | ............................... |
| ENTERTAINMENT | £ ................. | ............................... |
| OTHER COSTS | £ ................. | ............................... |

## TO DO TOMORROW

...............................................................
...............................................................
...............................................................
...............................................................

# NOTES

....................................................................................................

....................................................................................................

....................................................................................................

....................................................................................................

....................................................................................................

....................................................................................................

....................................................................................................

....................................................................................................

## SKETCH / KEEPSAKE / PHOTOGRAPH

# MOTORHOME
# TRAVEL JOURNAL

DATE ...................... MILEAGE START .........................

START TIME ............... MILEAGE END .........................

ARRIVAL TIME ............... MILEAGE TOTAL .........................

---

CAMPSITE NAME .........................................

ADDRESS 1 .........................................

ADDRESS 2 .........................................

POST CODE ..................... GPS .........................

E MAIL ......................... PHONE .........................

WEBSITE WWW .........................................

MY RATING ☆ ☆ ☆ ☆ ☆ NUMBER OF NIGHTS HERE ......

WEATHER ......................... TEMPERATURE .........................

---

## WILDCAMPING LOCATION NOTES

..................................................................

..................................................................

..................................................................

..................................................................

.............................................. GPS .........................

---

| DAILY COSTS | | TODAY'S HIGHLIGHTS |
|---|---|---|
| SITE FEES | £ ..................... | ......................... |
| FUEL | £ ..................... | ......................... |
| PROPANE | £ ..................... | ......................... |
| TOLLS | £ ..................... | ......................... |
| GROCERIES | £ ..................... | ......................... |
| DINING OUT | £ ..................... | ......................... |
| ENTERTAINMENT | £ ..................... | ......................... |
| OTHER COSTS | £ ..................... | |

## TO DO TOMORROW

..................................................................

..................................................................

..................................................................

..................................................................

# NOTES

SKETCH / KEEPSAKE / PHOTOGRAPH

# MOTORHOME
# TRAVEL JOURNAL

DATE ..................... MILEAGE START ........................

START TIME ............... MILEAGE END ........................

ARRIVAL TIME .............. MILEAGE TOTAL ........................

---

CAMPSITE NAME ........................................

ADDRESS I ........................................

ADDRESS 2 ........................................

POST CODE .................... GPS ........................

E MAIL ......................... PHONE ........................

WEBSITE WWW ........................................

MY RATING ☆ ☆ ☆ ☆ ☆ NUMBER OF NIGHTS HERE ......

WEATHER ......................... TEMPERATURE ........................

---

## WILDCAMPING LOCATION NOTES

........................................
........................................
........................................
........................................
.......................................... GPS ........................

---

## DAILY COSTS

SITE FEES £ .....................

FUEL £ .....................

PROPANE £ .....................

TOLLS £ .....................

GROCERIES £ .....................

DINING OUT £ .....................

ENTERTAINMENT £ .....................

OTHER COSTS £ .....................

## TODAY'S HIGHLIGHTS

........................
........................
........................
........................
........................
........................
........................

---

## TO DO TOMORROW

........................................

........................................

........................................

........................................

# NOTES

........................................................................................................

........................................................................................................

........................................................................................................

........................................................................................................

........................................................................................................

........................................................................................................

........................................................................................................

........................................................................................................

## SKETCH / KEEPSAKE / PHOTOGRAPH

# MOTORHOME
# TRAVEL JOURNAL

DATE ..................... MILEAGE START .....................

START TIME ............... MILEAGE END .....................

ARRIVAL TIME ............. MILEAGE TOTAL .....................

---

CAMPSITE NAME .............................................

ADDRESS 1 .................................................

ADDRESS 2 .................................................

POST CODE ................... GPS .........................

E MAIL ..................... PHONE ........................

WEBSITE WWW ...............................................

MY RATING ☆ ☆ ☆ ☆ ☆ NUMBER OF NIGHTS HERE ......

WEATHER ........................ TEMPERATURE .....................

---

## WILDCAMPING LOCATION NOTES

.............................................................
.............................................................
.............................................................
.............................................................
.............................. GPS .........................

---

| DAILY COSTS | TODAY'S HIGHLIGHTS |
|---|---|
| SITE FEES £ ................... | ................... |
| FUEL £ ................... | ................... |
| PROPANE £ ................... | ................... |
| TOLLS £ ................... | ................... |
| GROCERIES £ ................... | ................... |
| DINING OUT £ ................... | ................... |
| ENTERTAINMENT £ ................... | ................... |
| OTHER COSTS £ ................... | ................... |

## TO DO TOMORROW

.............................................................

.............................................................

.............................................................

.............................................................

# NOTES

..................................................................................

..................................................................................

..................................................................................

..................................................................................

..................................................................................

..................................................................................

..................................................................................

..................................................................................

## SKETCH / KEEPSAKE / PHOTOGRAPH

# MOTORHOME
# TRAVEL JOURNAL

DATE ...................... MILEAGE START ........................

START TIME .............. MILEAGE END .......................

ARRIVAL TIME .............. MILEAGE TOTAL .......................

---

CAMPSITE NAME ...............................................

ADDRESS 1 ...................................................

ADDRESS 2 ...................................................

POST CODE .................... GPS .............................

E MAIL ........................ PHONE ...........................

WEBSITE WWW ................................................

MY RATING ☆ ☆ ☆ ☆ ☆ NUMBER OF NIGHTS HERE ......

WEATHER .......................... TEMPERATURE ......................

---

## WILDCAMPING LOCATION NOTES

..................................................................
..................................................................
..................................................................
..................................................................
.............................. GPS ...............................

---

| DAILY COSTS | TODAY'S HIGHLIGHTS |
|---|---|
| SITE FEES £ ................ | ................................ |
| FUEL £ ................ | ................................ |
| PROPANE £ ................ | ................................ |
| TOLLS £ ................ | ................................ |
| GROCERIES £ ................ | ................................ |
| DINING OUT £ ................ | ................................ |
| ENTERTAINMENT £ ................ | ................................ |
| OTHER COSTS £ ................ | ................................ |

## TO DO TOMORROW

..................................................................
..................................................................
..................................................................
..................................................................

# NOTES

........................................................................................

........................................................................................

........................................................................................

........................................................................................

........................................................................................

........................................................................................

........................................................................................

## SKETCH / KEEPSAKE / PHOTOGRAPH

# MOTORHOME
# TRAVEL JOURNAL

DATE ..................... MILEAGE START ........................

START TIME ............... MILEAGE END ........................

ARRIVAL TIME ............... MILEAGE TOTAL ........................

CAMPSITE NAME ........................................

ADDRESS 1 ........................................

ADDRESS 2 ........................................

POST CODE ..................... GPS ........................

E MAIL ........................ PHONE ........................

WEBSITE WWW ........................................

MY RATING ☆ ☆ ☆ ☆ ☆ NUMBER OF NIGHTS HERE ......

WEATHER ........................ TEMPERATURE ..................

## WILDCAMPING LOCATION NOTES

........................................
........................................
........................................
........................................
........................... GPS ....................

| DAILY COSTS | | TODAY'S HIGHLIGHTS |
|---|---|---|
| SITE FEES | £ .................... | ............................ |
| FUEL | £ .................... | ............................ |
| PROPANE | £ .................... | ............................ |
| TOLLS | £ .................... | ............................ |
| GROCERIES | £ .................... | ............................ |
| DINING OUT | £ .................... | ............................ |
| ENTERTAINMENT | £ .................... | ............................ |
| OTHER COSTS | £ .................... | ............................ |

## TO DO TOMORROW

........................................
........................................
........................................
........................................

# NOTES

........................................................................................

........................................................................................

........................................................................................

........................................................................................

........................................................................................

........................................................................................

........................................................................................

........................................................................................

# SKETCH / KEEPSAKE / PHOTOGRAPH

# MOTORHOME
# TRAVEL JOURNAL

DATE .................... MILEAGE START ......................

START TIME .............. MILEAGE END ......................

ARRIVAL TIME ............ MILEAGE TOTAL ....................

---

CAMPSITE NAME ...........................................

ADDRESS 1 ...............................................

ADDRESS 2 ...............................................

POST CODE ................. GPS ........................

E MAIL .................. PHONE ..........................

WEBSITE WWW .............................................

MY RATING ☆ ☆ ☆ ☆ ☆  NUMBER OF NIGHTS HERE ......

WEATHER ...................... TEMPERATURE ..............

---

## WILDCAMPING LOCATION NOTES

...........................................................
...........................................................
...........................................................
...........................................................
.......................... GPS ............................

---

| DAILY COSTS | | TODAY'S HIGHLIGHTS |
|---|---|---|
| SITE FEES | £ ................ | ........................ |
| FUEL | £ ................ | ........................ |
| PROPANE | £ ................ | ........................ |
| TOLLS | £ ................ | ........................ |
| GROCERIES | £ ................ | ........................ |
| DINING OUT | £ ................ | ........................ |
| ENTERTAINMENT | £ ................ | ........................ |
| OTHER COSTS | £ ................ | |

## TO DO TOMORROW

...........................................................

...........................................................

...........................................................

...........................................................

# NOTES

................................................................................

................................................................................

................................................................................

................................................................................

................................................................................

................................................................................

................................................................................

................................................................................

## SKETCH / KEEPSAKE / PHOTOGRAPH

# MOTORHOME
# TRAVEL JOURNAL

DATE ..................... MILEAGE START ........................

START TIME ............... MILEAGE END ........................

ARRIVAL TIME ............ MILEAGE TOTAL ........................

CAMPSITE NAME ..............................................

ADDRESS 1 ..................................................

ADDRESS 2 ..................................................

POST CODE .................... GPS ...........................

E MAIL ....................... PHONE .........................

WEBSITE WWW ................................................

MY RATING ☆ ☆ ☆ ☆ ☆ NUMBER OF NIGHTS HERE ......

WEATHER ...................... TEMPERATURE ...................

## WILDCAMPING LOCATION NOTES

.................................................................

.................................................................

.................................................................

.................................................................

......................... GPS ...................................

## DAILY COSTS

SITE FEES £ .....................

FUEL £ .....................

PROPANE £ .....................

TOLLS £ .....................

GROCERIES £ .....................

DINING OUT £ .....................

ENTERTAINMENT £ .....................

OTHER COSTS £ .....................

## TODAY'S HIGHLIGHTS

.................................................

.................................................

.................................................

.................................................

.................................................

.................................................

.................................................

## TO DO TOMORROW

.................................................................

.................................................................

.................................................................

.................................................................

# NOTES

..........................................................................................

..........................................................................................

..........................................................................................

..........................................................................................

..........................................................................................

..........................................................................................

..........................................................................................

..........................................................................................

## SKETCH / KEEPSAKE / PHOTOGRAPH

# MOTORHOME
# TRAVEL JOURNAL

DATE ...................... MILEAGE START ........................

START TIME ................ MILEAGE END ........................

ARRIVAL TIME ................ MILEAGE TOTAL ........................

---

CAMPSITE NAME ........................................

ADDRESS 1 ........................................

ADDRESS 2 ........................................

POST CODE ...................... GPS ........................

E MAIL ........................ PHONE ........................

WEBSITE WWW ........................................

MY RATING ☆ ☆ ☆ ☆ ☆ NUMBER OF NIGHTS HERE ......

WEATHER ........................ TEMPERATURE ........................

---

## WILDCAMPING LOCATION NOTES

........................................

........................................

........................................

........................................

........................... GPS ........................

---

| DAILY COSTS | TODAY'S HIGHLIGHTS |
|---|---|
| SITE FEES £ ................ | ........................ |
| FUEL £ ................ | ........................ |
| PROPANE £ ................ | ........................ |
| TOLLS £ ................ | ........................ |
| GROCERIES £ ................ | ........................ |
| DINING OUT £ ................ | ........................ |
| ENTERTAINMENT £ ................ | ........................ |
| OTHER COSTS £ ................ | ........................ |

---

## TO DO TOMORROW

........................................

........................................

........................................

........................................

# NOTES

..........................................................................................................

..........................................................................................................

..........................................................................................................

..........................................................................................................

..........................................................................................................

..........................................................................................................

..........................................................................................................

..........................................................................................................

## SKETCH / KEEPSAKE / PHOTOGRAPH

# MOTORHOME
# TRAVEL JOURNAL

DATE ..................... MILEAGE START .........................

START TIME ................ MILEAGE END ........................

ARRIVAL TIME ............... MILEAGE TOTAL ........................

---

CAMPSITE NAME ...........................................................

ADDRESS I ...............................................................

ADDRESS 2 ...............................................................

POST CODE ..................... GPS ...................................

E MAIL ........................ PHONE .................................

WEBSITE WWW ...........................................................

MY RATING ☆ ☆ ☆ ☆ ☆ NUMBER OF NIGHTS HERE ......

WEATHER .......................... TEMPERATURE ......................

---

### WILDCAMPING LOCATION NOTES

...........................................................................
...........................................................................
...........................................................................
...........................................................................
.................................... GPS ..................................

---

| DAILY COSTS | | TODAY'S HIGHLIGHTS |
|---|---|---|
| SITE FEES | £ .................... | ............................... |
| FUEL | £ .................... | ............................... |
| PROPANE | £ .................... | ............................... |
| TOLLS | £ .................... | ............................... |
| GROCERIES | £ .................... | ............................... |
| DINING OUT | £ .................... | ............................... |
| ENTERTAINMENT | £ .................... | ............................... |
| OTHER COSTS | £ .................... | ............................... |

### TO DO TOMORROW

...........................................................................
...........................................................................
...........................................................................
...........................................................................

# NOTES

........................................................................................................

........................................................................................................

........................................................................................................

........................................................................................................

........................................................................................................

........................................................................................................

........................................................................................................

........................................................................................................

## SKETCH / KEEPSAKE / PHOTOGRAPH

# MOTORHOME
# TRAVEL JOURNAL

DATE ..................... MILEAGE START ........................

START TIME ............... MILEAGE END ........................

ARRIVAL TIME ................ MILEAGE TOTAL ......................

---

CAMPSITE NAME ............................................

ADDRESS 1 ................................................

ADDRESS 2 ................................................

POST CODE ..................... GPS ........................

E MAIL ......................... PHONE ......................

WEBSITE WWW ..............................................

MY RATING ☆ ☆ ☆ ☆ ☆ NUMBER OF NIGHTS HERE ......

WEATHER ......................... TEMPERATURE ......................

---

## WILDCAMPING LOCATION NOTES

..........................................................
..........................................................
..........................................................
..........................................................
........................................ GPS ......................

---

## DAILY COSTS

SITE FEES £ ......................

FUEL £ ......................

PROPANE £ ......................

TOLLS £ ......................

GROCERIES £ ......................

DINING OUT £ ......................

ENTERTAINMENT £ ......................

OTHER COSTS £ ......................

## TODAY'S HIGHLIGHTS

..................................
..................................
..................................
..................................
..................................
..................................
..................................

## TO DO TOMORROW

..........................................................
..........................................................
..........................................................
..........................................................

# NOTES

..............................................................................................................

..............................................................................................................

..............................................................................................................

..............................................................................................................

..............................................................................................................

..............................................................................................................

..............................................................................................................

..............................................................................................................

## SKETCH / KEEPSAKE / PHOTOGRAPH

# MOTORHOME
# TRAVEL JOURNAL

DATE ...................... MILEAGE START ........................

START TIME ................ MILEAGE END ........................

ARRIVAL TIME .............. MILEAGE TOTAL ......................

CAMPSITE NAME ....................................................

ADDRESS 1 ........................................................

ADDRESS 2 ........................................................

POST CODE ...................... GPS ..............................

E MAIL ......................... PHONE ............................

WEBSITE WWW ......................................................

MY RATING ☆ ☆ ☆ ☆ ☆ NUMBER OF NIGHTS HERE ......

WEATHER .......................... TEMPERATURE ....................

## WILDCAMPING LOCATION NOTES

...................................................................

...................................................................

...................................................................

...................................................................

........................................ GPS ......................

## DAILY COSTS

SITE FEES £ .....................

FUEL £ .....................

PROPANE £ .....................

TOLLS £ .....................

GROCERIES £ .....................

DINING OUT £ .....................

ENTERTAINMENT £ .....................

OTHER COSTS £ .....................

## TODAY'S HIGHLIGHTS

...................................................

...................................................

...................................................

...................................................

...................................................

...................................................

...................................................

## TO DO TOMORROW

...................................................................

...................................................................

...................................................................

...................................................................

# NOTES

......................................................................................................

......................................................................................................

......................................................................................................

......................................................................................................

......................................................................................................

......................................................................................................

......................................................................................................

......................................................................................................

## SKETCH / KEEPSAKE / PHOTOGRAPH

# MOTORHOME
# TRAVEL JOURNAL

DATE .................... MILEAGE START ......................

START TIME ............... MILEAGE END .......................

ARRIVAL TIME ............. MILEAGE TOTAL .......................

---

CAMPSITE NAME ..........................................

ADDRESS 1 ..............................................

ADDRESS 2 ..............................................

POST CODE .................... GPS ....................................

E MAIL ........................ PHONE ..............................

WEBSITE WWW ........................................

MY RATING ☆ ☆ ☆ ☆ ☆ NUMBER OF NIGHTS HERE ......

WEATHER ......................... TEMPERATURE ......................

---

## WILDCAMPING LOCATION NOTES

...........................................................
...........................................................
...........................................................
...........................................................
.............................. GPS ...............................

---

| DAILY COSTS | | TODAY'S HIGHLIGHTS |
|---|---|---|
| SITE FEES | £ .................... | ................................ |
| FUEL | £ .................... | ................................ |
| PROPANE | £ .................... | ................................ |
| TOLLS | £ .................... | ................................ |
| GROCERIES | £ .................... | ................................ |
| DINING OUT | £ .................... | ................................ |
| ENTERTAINMENT | £ .................... | ................................ |
| OTHER COSTS | £ .................... | ................................ |

## TO DO TOMORROW

...........................................................
...........................................................
...........................................................
...........................................................

# NOTES

........................................................................

........................................................................

........................................................................

........................................................................

........................................................................

........................................................................

........................................................................

........................................................................

## SKETCH / KEEPSAKE / PHOTOGRAPH

# MOTORHOME
# TRAVEL JOURNAL

DATE ..................... MILEAGE START ........................

START TIME .............. MILEAGE END ........................

ARRIVAL TIME ........... MILEAGE TOTAL ........................

---

CAMPSITE NAME ............................................

ADDRESS 1 ..................................................

ADDRESS 2 ..................................................

POST CODE .................... GPS ........................

E MAIL ........................ PHONE ........................

WEBSITE WWW ...............................................

MY RATING ☆ ☆ ☆ ☆ ☆  NUMBER OF NIGHTS HERE ......

WEATHER ......................... TEMPERATURE ....................

---

## WILDCAMPING LOCATION NOTES

................................................................
................................................................
................................................................
................................................................
........................... GPS ................................

---

## DAILY COSTS

| | | |
|---|---|---|
| SITE FEES | £ | ..................... |
| FUEL | £ | ..................... |
| PROPANE | £ | ..................... |
| TOLLS | £ | ..................... |
| GROCERIES | £ | ..................... |
| DINING OUT | £ | ..................... |
| ENTERTAINMENT | £ | ..................... |
| OTHER COSTS | £ | ..................... |

## TODAY'S HIGHLIGHTS

................................
................................
................................
................................
................................
................................
................................

## TO DO TOMORROW

................................................................
................................................................
................................................................
................................................................

# NOTES

........................................................................................

........................................................................................

........................................................................................

........................................................................................

........................................................................................

........................................................................................

........................................................................................

........................................................................................

## SKETCH / KEEPSAKE / PHOTOGRAPH

# MOTORHOME
# TRAVEL JOURNAL

DATE ...................... MILEAGE START ........................

START TIME ................ MILEAGE END ........................

ARRIVAL TIME ................ MILEAGE TOTAL ........................

---

CAMPSITE NAME ........................................

ADDRESS 1 ........................................

ADDRESS 2 ........................................

POST CODE ...................... GPS ........................

E MAIL ........................ PHONE ........................

WEBSITE WWW ........................................

MY RATING ☆ ☆ ☆ ☆ ☆ NUMBER OF NIGHTS HERE ......

WEATHER ........................ TEMPERATURE ........................

---

## WILDCAMPING LOCATION NOTES

........................................................

........................................................

........................................................

........................................................

............................ GPS ........................

---

| DAILY COSTS | | TODAY'S HIGHLIGHTS |
|---|---|---|
| SITE FEES | £ .................. | ........................ |
| FUEL | £ .................. | ........................ |
| PROPANE | £ .................. | ........................ |
| TOLLS | £ .................. | ........................ |
| GROCERIES | £ .................. | ........................ |
| DINING OUT | £ .................. | ........................ |
| ENTERTAINMENT | £ .................. | ........................ |
| OTHER COSTS | £ .................. | ........................ |

---

## TO DO TOMORROW

........................................................

........................................................

........................................................

........................................................

# NOTES

..........................................................................................

..........................................................................................

..........................................................................................

..........................................................................................

..........................................................................................

..........................................................................................

..........................................................................................

..........................................................................................

## SKETCH / KEEPSAKE / PHOTOGRAPH

# MOTORHOME
# TRAVEL JOURNAL

DATE ..................... MILEAGE START .........................

START TIME ............... MILEAGE END .........................

ARRIVAL TIME ............... MILEAGE TOTAL .........................

---

CAMPSITE NAME ...............................................

ADDRESS 1 ...................................................

ADDRESS 2 ...................................................

POST CODE .................... GPS ...........................

E MAIL ......................... PHONE .......................

WEBSITE WWW .................................................

MY RATING ☆  ☆  ☆  ☆  ☆  NUMBER OF NIGHTS HERE ......

WEATHER ......................... TEMPERATURE .................

---

## WILDCAMPING LOCATION NOTES

..............................................................
..............................................................
..............................................................
..............................................................
.............................. GPS ...........................

---

| DAILY COSTS | | TODAY'S HIGHLIGHTS |
|---|---|---|
| SITE FEES | £ ................. | ................................. |
| FUEL | £ ................. | ................................. |
| PROPANE | £ ................. | ................................. |
| TOLLS | £ ................. | ................................. |
| GROCERIES | £ ................. | ................................. |
| DINING OUT | £ ................. | ................................. |
| ENTERTAINMENT | £ ................. | ................................. |
| OTHER COSTS | £ ................. | |

## TO DO TOMORROW

..............................................................
..............................................................
..............................................................
..............................................................

# NOTES

........................................................................................

........................................................................................

........................................................................................

........................................................................................

........................................................................................

........................................................................................

........................................................................................

........................................................................................

## SKETCH / KEEPSAKE / PHOTOGRAPH

# MOTORHOME
# TRAVEL JOURNAL

DATE ..................... MILEAGE START ........................

START TIME ............... MILEAGE END ........................

ARRIVAL TIME ............... MILEAGE TOTAL ........................

---

CAMPSITE NAME ............................................

ADDRESS 1 ................................................

ADDRESS 2 ................................................

POST CODE ..................... GPS ........................

E MAIL ........................ PHONE ......................

WEBSITE WWW ..............................................

MY RATING ☆ ☆ ☆ ☆ ☆    NUMBER OF NIGHTS HERE ......

WEATHER ......................... TEMPERATURE ......................

---

## WILDCAMPING LOCATION NOTES

......................................................

......................................................

......................................................

......................................................

......................................... GPS ......................

---

| DAILY COSTS | | TODAY'S HIGHLIGHTS |
|---|---|---|
| SITE FEES | £ ..................... | ................................ |
| FUEL | £ ..................... | ................................ |
| PROPANE | £ ..................... | ................................ |
| TOLLS | £ ..................... | ................................ |
| GROCERIES | £ ..................... | ................................ |
| DINING OUT | £ ..................... | ................................ |
| ENTERTAINMENT | £ ..................... | ................................ |
| OTHER COSTS | £ ..................... | ................................ |

## TO DO TOMORROW

......................................................

......................................................

......................................................

......................................................

# NOTES

............................................................................................

............................................................................................

............................................................................................

............................................................................................

............................................................................................

............................................................................................

............................................................................................

............................................................................................

## SKETCH / KEEPSAKE / PHOTOGRAPH

# MOTORHOME
# TRAVEL JOURNAL

DATE ...................... MILEAGE START ........................

START TIME ................ MILEAGE END ........................

ARRIVAL TIME ............... MILEAGE TOTAL ........................

CAMPSITE NAME ....................................................

ADDRESS 1 .......................................................

ADDRESS 2 .......................................................

POST CODE ..................... GPS ............................

E MAIL ........................ PHONE ..........................

WEBSITE WWW .....................................................

MY RATING ☆ ☆ ☆ ☆ ☆ NUMBER OF NIGHTS HERE ......

WEATHER .......................... TEMPERATURE ....................

## WILDCAMPING LOCATION NOTES

..................................................................
..................................................................
..................................................................
..................................................................
............................... GPS ..............................

| DAILY COSTS | | TODAY'S HIGHLIGHTS |
|---|---|---|
| SITE FEES | £ ................... | ........................... |
| FUEL | £ ................... | ........................... |
| PROPANE | £ ................... | ........................... |
| TOLLS | £ ................... | ........................... |
| GROCERIES | £ ................... | ........................... |
| DINING OUT | £ ................... | ........................... |
| ENTERTAINMENT | £ ................... | ........................... |
| OTHER COSTS | £ ................... | ........................... |

## TO DO TOMORROW

..................................................................
..................................................................
..................................................................
..................................................................

# NOTES

........................................................................................

........................................................................................

........................................................................................

........................................................................................

........................................................................................

........................................................................................

........................................................................................

........................................................................................

## SKETCH / KEEPSAKE / PHOTOGRAPH

# MOTORHOME
# TRAVEL JOURNAL

DATE ..................... MILEAGE START .......................

START TIME .............. MILEAGE END .......................

ARRIVAL TIME .............. MILEAGE TOTAL .......................

---

CAMPSITE NAME ...........................................

ADDRESS 1 ...............................................

ADDRESS 2 ...............................................

POST CODE .................... GPS ..........................

E MAIL ......................... PHONE .......................

WEBSITE WWW ............................................

MY RATING ☆ ☆ ☆ ☆ ☆ NUMBER OF NIGHTS HERE ......

WEATHER ......................... TEMPERATURE .......................

---

## WILDCAMPING LOCATION NOTES

...........................................................
...........................................................
...........................................................
...........................................................
.................................. GPS .......................

---

| DAILY COSTS | | TODAY'S HIGHLIGHTS |
|---|---|---|
| SITE FEES | £ ..................... | ............................. |
| FUEL | £ ..................... | ............................. |
| PROPANE | £ ..................... | ............................. |
| TOLLS | £ ..................... | ............................. |
| GROCERIES | £ ..................... | ............................. |
| DINING OUT | £ ..................... | ............................. |
| ENTERTAINMENT | £ ..................... | ............................. |
| OTHER COSTS | £ ..................... | ............................. |

## TO DO TOMORROW

...........................................................
...........................................................
...........................................................
...........................................................

# NOTES

........................................................................................................

........................................................................................................

........................................................................................................

........................................................................................................

........................................................................................................

........................................................................................................

........................................................................................................

........................................................................................................

## SKETCH / KEEPSAKE / PHOTOGRAPH

# MOTORHOME
# TRAVEL JOURNAL

DATE ..................... MILEAGE START .........................

START TIME ............... MILEAGE END .......................

ARRIVAL TIME ............... MILEAGE TOTAL ......................

---

CAMPSITE NAME ........................................

ADDRESS 1 ........................................

ADDRESS 2 ........................................

POST CODE ..................... GPS ..............................

E MAIL ........................... PHONE ..........................

WEBSITE WWW ........................................

MY RATING ☆ ☆ ☆ ☆ ☆ NUMBER OF NIGHTS HERE ......

WEATHER .......................... TEMPERATURE ......................

---

## WILDCAMPING LOCATION NOTES

..........................................................................

..........................................................................

..........................................................................

..........................................................................

.............................. GPS ......................................

---

| DAILY COSTS | | TODAY'S HIGHLIGHTS |
|---|---|---|
| SITE FEES | £ ..................... | ............................. |
| FUEL | £ ..................... | ............................. |
| PROPANE | £ ..................... | ............................. |
| TOLLS | £ ..................... | ............................. |
| GROCERIES | £ ..................... | ............................. |
| DINING OUT | £ ..................... | ............................. |
| ENTERTAINMENT | £ ..................... | ............................. |
| OTHER COSTS | £ ..................... | ............................. |

## TO DO TOMORROW

..........................................................................

..........................................................................

..........................................................................

..........................................................................

# NOTES

........................................................................................

........................................................................................

........................................................................................

........................................................................................

........................................................................................

........................................................................................

........................................................................................

## SKETCH / KEEPSAKE / PHOTOGRAPH

# MOTORHOME
# TRAVEL JOURNAL

DATE ...................... MILEAGE START ......................

START TIME ............... MILEAGE END ......................

ARRIVAL TIME ............ MILEAGE TOTAL ......................

CAMPSITE NAME ...........................................

ADDRESS 1 ..................................................

ADDRESS 2 ..................................................

POST CODE ..................... GPS ...........................

E MAIL ......................... PHONE ........................

WEBSITE WWW ............................................

MY RATING ☆ ☆ ☆ ☆ ☆ NUMBER OF NIGHTS HERE ......

WEATHER .......................... TEMPERATURE ....................

## WILDCAMPING LOCATION NOTES

......................................................

......................................................

......................................................

......................................................

.............................. GPS .......................

| DAILY COSTS | | TODAY'S HIGHLIGHTS |
|---|---|---|
| SITE FEES | £ ............... | ................................ |
| FUEL | £ ............... | ................................ |
| PROPANE | £ ............... | ................................ |
| TOLLS | £ ............... | ................................ |
| GROCERIES | £ ............... | ................................ |
| DINING OUT | £ ............... | ................................ |
| ENTERTAINMENT | £ ............... | ................................ |
| OTHER COSTS | £ ............... | ................................ |

## TO DO TOMORROW

......................................................

......................................................

......................................................

......................................................

# NOTES

......................................................................................................

......................................................................................................

......................................................................................................

......................................................................................................

......................................................................................................

......................................................................................................

......................................................................................................

......................................................................................................

## SKETCH / KEEPSAKE / PHOTOGRAPH

# MOTORHOME
# TRAVEL JOURNAL

DATE ..................... MILEAGE START .......................

START TIME ............... MILEAGE END ........................

ARRIVAL TIME ............. MILEAGE TOTAL ......................

---

CAMPSITE NAME ...........................................

ADDRESS 1 ...............................................

ADDRESS 2 ...............................................

POST CODE .................... GPS ......................

E MAIL ....................... PHONE ....................

WEBSITE WWW .............................................

MY RATING ☆ ☆ ☆ ☆ ☆   NUMBER OF NIGHTS HERE ......

WEATHER ..................... TEMPERATURE ...............

---

## WILDCAMPING LOCATION NOTES

.........................................................
.........................................................
.........................................................
.........................................................
................................ GPS ....................

---

| DAILY COSTS | TODAY'S HIGHLIGHTS |
|---|---|
| SITE FEES £ ................. | ........................... |
| FUEL £ ................. | ........................... |
| PROPANE £ ................. | ........................... |
| TOLLS £ ................. | ........................... |
| GROCERIES £ ................. | ........................... |
| DINING OUT £ ................. | ........................... |
| ENTERTAINMENT £ ................. | ........................... |
| OTHER COSTS £ ................. | ........................... |

## TO DO TOMORROW

.........................................................

.........................................................

.........................................................

.........................................................

# NOTES

SKETCH / KEEPSAKE / PHOTOGRAPH

# MOTORHOME
# TRAVEL JOURNAL

DATE ...................... MILEAGE START .........................

START TIME ............... MILEAGE END .........................

ARRIVAL TIME ............. MILEAGE TOTAL .......................

---

CAMPSITE NAME ...............................................

ADDRESS 1 ...................................................

ADDRESS 2 ...................................................

POST CODE ..................... GPS .........................

E MAIL .......................... PHONE ......................

WEBSITE WWW ................................................

MY RATING ☆ ☆ ☆ ☆ ☆ NUMBER OF NIGHTS HERE ......

WEATHER .......................... TEMPERATURE ...............

---

## WILDCAMPING LOCATION NOTES

.............................................................
.............................................................
.............................................................
.............................................................
............................... GPS ........................

---

## DAILY COSTS

| | | | TODAY'S HIGHLIGHTS |
|---|---|---|---|
| SITE FEES | £ .................... | | ........................... |
| FUEL | £ .................... | | ........................... |
| PROPANE | £ .................... | | ........................... |
| TOLLS | £ .................... | | ........................... |
| GROCERIES | £ .................... | | ........................... |
| DINING OUT | £ .................... | | ........................... |
| ENTERTAINMENT | £ .................... | | ........................... |
| OTHER COSTS | £ .................... | | |

## TO DO TOMORROW

.............................................................

.............................................................

.............................................................

.............................................................

# NOTES

.......................................................................................................

.......................................................................................................

.......................................................................................................

.......................................................................................................

.......................................................................................................

.......................................................................................................

.......................................................................................................

.......................................................................................................

## SKETCH / KEEPSAKE / PHOTOGRAPH

# MOTORHOME
# TRAVEL JOURNAL

DATE ....................... MILEAGE START ........................

START TIME ................ MILEAGE END ........................

ARRIVAL TIME ............... MILEAGE TOTAL ........................

CAMPSITE NAME ........................................................

ADDRESS 1 ...........................................................

ADDRESS 2 ...........................................................

POST CODE ...................... GPS ................................

E MAIL ........................... PHONE .............................

WEBSITE WWW .......................................................

MY RATING ☆ ☆ ☆ ☆ ☆ NUMBER OF NIGHTS HERE ......

WEATHER ........................... TEMPERATURE ......................

## WILDCAMPING LOCATION NOTES

..................................................................

..................................................................

..................................................................

..................................................................

............................... GPS ..............................

## DAILY COSTS

| | | |
|---|---|---|
| SITE FEES | £ | ................ |
| FUEL | £ | ................ |
| PROPANE | £ | ................ |
| TOLLS | £ | ................ |
| GROCERIES | £ | ................ |
| DINING OUT | £ | ................ |
| ENTERTAINMENT | £ | ................ |
| OTHER COSTS | £ | ................ |

## TODAY'S HIGHLIGHTS

................................................

................................................

................................................

................................................

................................................

................................................

................................................

## TO DO TOMORROW

..................................................................

..................................................................

..................................................................

..................................................................

# NOTES

........................................................................................................

........................................................................................................

........................................................................................................

........................................................................................................

........................................................................................................

........................................................................................................

........................................................................................................

........................................................................................................

## SKETCH / KEEPSAKE / PHOTOGRAPH

# MOTORHOME
# TRAVEL JOURNAL

DATE ..................... MILEAGE START .......................

START TIME ............... MILEAGE END .......................

ARRIVAL TIME ............. MILEAGE TOTAL .......................

---

CAMPSITE NAME ...........................................

ADDRESS 1 ...............................................

ADDRESS 2 ...............................................

POST CODE .................... GPS ........................

E MAIL ....................... PHONE ......................

WEBSITE WWW .............................................

MY RATING ☆ ☆ ☆ ☆ ☆ NUMBER OF NIGHTS HERE ......

WEATHER ...................... TEMPERATURE .................

---

### WILDCAMPING LOCATION NOTES

......................................................
......................................................
......................................................
......................................................
......................................... GPS ...................................

---

| DAILY COSTS | TODAY'S HIGHLIGHTS |
|---|---|
| SITE FEES £ ..................... | ..................................... |
| FUEL £ ..................... | ..................................... |
| PROPANE £ ..................... | ..................................... |
| TOLLS £ ..................... | ..................................... |
| GROCERIES £ ..................... | ..................................... |
| DINING OUT £ ..................... | ..................................... |
| ENTERTAINMENT £ ..................... | ..................................... |
| OTHER COSTS £ ..................... | ..................................... |

### TO DO TOMORROW

......................................................
......................................................
......................................................
......................................................

# NOTES

............................................................................................

............................................................................................

............................................................................................

............................................................................................

............................................................................................

............................................................................................

............................................................................................

............................................................................................

## SKETCH / KEEPSAKE / PHOTOGRAPH

# MOTORHOME
# TRAVEL JOURNAL

DATE ..................... MILEAGE START ........................

START TIME ............... MILEAGE END ........................

ARRIVAL TIME ............. MILEAGE TOTAL ........................

---

CAMPSITE NAME ........................................

ADDRESS 1 ........................................

ADDRESS 2 ........................................

POST CODE .................... GPS ........................

E MAIL ........................ PHONE ........................

WEBSITE WWW ........................................

MY RATING ☆ ☆ ☆ ☆ ☆ NUMBER OF NIGHTS HERE ......

WEATHER ........................ TEMPERATURE ........................

---

## WILDCAMPING LOCATION NOTES

........................................

........................................

........................................

........................................

.............................. GPS ........................

---

| DAILY COSTS | | TODAY'S HIGHLIGHTS |
|---|---|---|
| SITE FEES | £ ............... | ........................ |
| FUEL | £ ............... | ........................ |
| PROPANE | £ ............... | ........................ |
| TOLLS | £ ............... | ........................ |
| GROCERIES | £ ............... | ........................ |
| DINING OUT | £ ............... | ........................ |
| ENTERTAINMENT | £ ............... | ........................ |
| OTHER COSTS | £ ............... | ........................ |

## TO DO TOMORROW

........................................

........................................

........................................

........................................

# NOTES

........................................................................................

........................................................................................

........................................................................................

........................................................................................

........................................................................................

........................................................................................

........................................................................................

## SKETCH / KEEPSAKE / PHOTOGRAPH

# MOTORHOME
# TRAVEL JOURNAL

DATE ...................... MILEAGE START ........................

START TIME ................ MILEAGE END .......................

ARRIVAL TIME ............... MILEAGE TOTAL .......................

---

CAMPSITE NAME ....................................................

ADDRESS 1 .......................................................

ADDRESS 2 .......................................................

POST CODE ..................... GPS ..............................

E MAIL ......................... PHONE ...........................

WEBSITE WWW .....................................................

MY RATING ☆ ☆ ☆ ☆ ☆ NUMBER OF NIGHTS HERE ......

WEATHER ......................... TEMPERATURE ....................

---

## WILDCAMPING LOCATION NOTES

........................................................................

........................................................................

........................................................................

........................................................................

.............................. GPS ....................................

---

## DAILY COSTS

| | | TODAY'S HIGHLIGHTS |
|---|---|---|

SITE FEES £ ...................

FUEL £ ...................

PROPANE £ ...................

TOLLS £ ...................

GROCERIES £ ...................

DINING OUT £ ...................

ENTERTAINMENT £ ...................

OTHER COSTS £ ...................

## TODAY'S HIGHLIGHTS

....................................

....................................

....................................

....................................

....................................

....................................

....................................

---

## TO DO TOMORROW

........................................................................

........................................................................

........................................................................

........................................................................

# NOTES

..............................................................................................................

..............................................................................................................

..............................................................................................................

..............................................................................................................

..............................................................................................................

..............................................................................................................

..............................................................................................................

## SKETCH / KEEPSAKE / PHOTOGRAPH

# MOTORHOME
# TRAVEL JOURNAL

DATE ..................... MILEAGE START .......................

START TIME ............... MILEAGE END ........................

ARRIVAL TIME ............. MILEAGE TOTAL ......................

---

CAMPSITE NAME ...........................................

ADDRESS 1 ...............................................

ADDRESS 2 ...............................................

POST CODE .................... GPS ......................

E MAIL ........................ PHONE ...................

WEBSITE WWW ............................................

MY RATING ☆ ☆ ☆ ☆ ☆ NUMBER OF NIGHTS HERE ......

WEATHER ......................... TEMPERATURE ...............

---

## WILDCAMPING LOCATION NOTES

.............................................................
.............................................................
.............................................................
.............................................................
.......................... GPS ..............................

---

| DAILY COSTS | TODAY'S HIGHLIGHTS |
|---|---|
| SITE FEES £ ................. | ....................... |
| FUEL £ ................. | ....................... |
| PROPANE £ ................. | ....................... |
| TOLLS £ ................. | ....................... |
| GROCERIES £ ................. | ....................... |
| DINING OUT £ ................. | ....................... |
| ENTERTAINMENT £ ................. | ....................... |
| OTHER COSTS £ ................. | ....................... |

## TO DO TOMORROW

.............................................................

.............................................................

.............................................................

.............................................................

# NOTES

_____

_____

_____

_____

_____

_____

_____

## SKETCH / KEEPSAKE / PHOTOGRAPH

# MOTORHOME
# TRAVEL JOURNAL

DATE ...................... MILEAGE START ........................

START TIME .............. MILEAGE END .......................

ARRIVAL TIME ............... MILEAGE TOTAL .......................

---

CAMPSITE NAME .......................................................

ADDRESS 1 ...........................................................

ADDRESS 2 ...........................................................

POST CODE ...................... GPS ...............................

E MAIL ........................... PHONE ...............................

WEBSITE WWW .........................................................

MY RATING ☆ ☆ ☆ ☆ ☆ NUMBER OF NIGHTS HERE ......

WEATHER ........................... TEMPERATURE .......................

---

## WILDCAMPING LOCATION NOTES

...........................................................
...........................................................
...........................................................
...........................................................
........................... GPS ...............................

---

| DAILY COSTS | TODAY'S HIGHLIGHTS |
|---|---|
| SITE FEES £ ..................... | ................................ |
| FUEL £ ..................... | ................................ |
| PROPANE £ ..................... | ................................ |
| TOLLS £ ..................... | ................................ |
| GROCERIES £ ..................... | ................................ |
| DINING OUT £ ..................... | ................................ |
| ENTERTAINMENT £ ..................... | ................................ |
| OTHER COSTS £ ..................... | |

## TO DO TOMORROW

...........................................................
...........................................................
...........................................................
...........................................................

# NOTES

........................................................................................................

........................................................................................................

........................................................................................................

........................................................................................................

........................................................................................................

........................................................................................................

........................................................................................................

## SKETCH / KEEPSAKE / PHOTOGRAPH

# MOTORHOME
# TRAVEL JOURNAL

DATE ...................... MILEAGE START ........................

START TIME ................ MILEAGE END ........................

ARRIVAL TIME ............... MILEAGE TOTAL ........................

CAMPSITE NAME ..........................................................

ADDRESS 1 ..............................................................

ADDRESS 2 ..............................................................

POST CODE ...................... GPS .....................................

E MAIL ......................... PHONE ...................................

WEBSITE WWW ...........................................................

MY RATING ☆ ☆ ☆ ☆ ☆ NUMBER OF NIGHTS HERE ......

WEATHER ......................... TEMPERATURE ......................

## WILDCAMPING LOCATION NOTES

..............................................................................
..............................................................................
..............................................................................
..............................................................................
........................................ GPS ..................................

| DAILY COSTS | | TODAY'S HIGHLIGHTS |
|---|---|---|
| SITE FEES | £ .................. | .................................... |
| FUEL | £ .................. | .................................... |
| PROPANE | £ .................. | .................................... |
| TOLLS | £ .................. | .................................... |
| GROCERIES | £ .................. | .................................... |
| DINING OUT | £ .................. | .................................... |
| ENTERTAINMENT | £ .................. | .................................... |
| OTHER COSTS | £ .................. | .................................... |

## TO DO TOMORROW

..............................................................................

..............................................................................

..............................................................................

..............................................................................

# NOTES

........................................................................................................

........................................................................................................

........................................................................................................

........................................................................................................

........................................................................................................

........................................................................................................

........................................................................................................

........................................................................................................

## SKETCH / KEEPSAKE / PHOTOGRAPH

# MOTORHOME
# TRAVEL JOURNAL

DATE ..................... MILEAGE START ......................

START TIME ............... MILEAGE END .......................

ARRIVAL TIME ............. MILEAGE TOTAL ......................

---

CAMPSITE NAME ..............................................

ADDRESS 1 ..................................................

ADDRESS 2 ..................................................

POST CODE ..................... GPS ........................

E MAIL ......................... PHONE .....................

WEBSITE WWW ................................................

MY RATING ☆ ☆ ☆ ☆ ☆ NUMBER OF NIGHTS HERE ......

WEATHER .......................... TEMPERATURE .....................

---

## WILDCAMPING LOCATION NOTES

.............................................................
.............................................................
.............................................................
.............................................................
.................................. GPS ......................

---

## DAILY COSTS

## TODAY'S HIGHLIGHTS

SITE FEES £ ....................

FUEL £ ....................

PROPANE £ ....................

TOLLS £ ....................

GROCERIES £ ....................

DINING OUT £ ....................

ENTERTAINMENT £ ....................

OTHER COSTS £ ....................

## TO DO TOMORROW

.............................................................

.............................................................

.............................................................

.............................................................

# NOTES

........................................................................................................

........................................................................................................

........................................................................................................

........................................................................................................

........................................................................................................

........................................................................................................

........................................................................................................

## SKETCH / KEEPSAKE / PHOTOGRAPH

# MOTORHOME
# TRAVEL JOURNAL

DATE ..................... MILEAGE START .........................

START TIME ............... MILEAGE END ........................

ARRIVAL TIME ............... MILEAGE TOTAL ......................

CAMPSITE NAME ..............................................

ADDRESS 1 .................................................

ADDRESS 2 .................................................

POST CODE ..................... GPS ........................

E MAIL .......................... PHONE .....................

WEBSITE WWW ................................................

MY RATING ☆ ☆ ☆ ☆ ☆ NUMBER OF NIGHTS HERE ......

WEATHER .......................... TEMPERATURE .....................

## WILDCAMPING LOCATION NOTES

..........................................................
..........................................................
..........................................................
..........................................................
........................... GPS ...........................

## DAILY COSTS

SITE FEES £ ..................

FUEL £ ..................

PROPANE £ ..................

TOLLS £ ..................

GROCERIES £ ..................

DINING OUT £ ..................

ENTERTAINMENT £ ..................

OTHER COSTS £ ..................

## TODAY'S HIGHLIGHTS

..........................................
..........................................
..........................................
..........................................
..........................................
..........................................
..........................................

## TO DO TOMORROW

..........................................................
..........................................................
..........................................................
..........................................................

# NOTES

........................................................................................................

........................................................................................................

........................................................................................................

........................................................................................................

........................................................................................................

........................................................................................................

........................................................................................................

........................................................................................................

## SKETCH / KEEPSAKE / PHOTOGRAPH

# MOTORHOME
# TRAVEL JOURNAL

DATE ...................... MILEAGE START .........................

START TIME ............... MILEAGE END .........................

ARRIVAL TIME ............. MILEAGE TOTAL .........................

---

CAMPSITE NAME ..............................................

ADDRESS 1 ...................................................

ADDRESS 2 ...................................................

POST CODE ..................... GPS .........................

E MAIL ........................ PHONE ........................

WEBSITE WWW ................................................

MY RATING ☆ ☆ ☆ ☆ ☆ NUMBER OF NIGHTS HERE ......

WEATHER .......................... TEMPERATURE ....................

---

## WILDCAMPING LOCATION NOTES

..............................................................
..............................................................
..............................................................
..............................................................
......................................... GPS ....................

| DAILY COSTS | TODAY'S HIGHLIGHTS |
|---|---|
| SITE FEES £ ..................... | ............................. |
| FUEL £ ..................... | ............................. |
| PROPANE £ ..................... | ............................. |
| TOLLS £ ..................... | ............................. |
| GROCERIES £ ..................... | ............................. |
| DINING OUT £ ..................... | ............................. |
| ENTERTAINMENT £ ..................... | ............................. |
| OTHER COSTS £ ..................... | ............................. |

## TO DO TOMORROW

..............................................................

..............................................................

..............................................................

..............................................................

# NOTES

........................................................................................

........................................................................................

........................................................................................

........................................................................................

........................................................................................

........................................................................................

........................................................................................

........................................................................................

## SKETCH / KEEPSAKE / PHOTOGRAPH

# MOTORHOME
# TRAVEL JOURNAL

DATE ..................... MILEAGE START ........................

START TIME .............. MILEAGE END ........................

ARRIVAL TIME ............. MILEAGE TOTAL ........................

---

CAMPSITE NAME ...............................................

ADDRESS 1 ...................................................

ADDRESS 2 ...................................................

POST CODE .................... GPS ...........................

E MAIL .......................... PHONE .......................

WEBSITE WWW .................................................

MY RATING ☆ ☆ ☆ ☆ ☆ NUMBER OF NIGHTS HERE ......

WEATHER ......................... TEMPERATURE .................

---

## WILDCAMPING LOCATION NOTES

...............................................................
...............................................................
...............................................................
...............................................................
............................... GPS ...........................

---

## DAILY COSTS

| | |
|---|---|
| SITE FEES | £ ..................... |
| FUEL | £ ..................... |
| PROPANE | £ ..................... |
| TOLLS | £ ..................... |
| GROCERIES | £ ..................... |
| DINING OUT | £ ..................... |
| ENTERTAINMENT | £ ..................... |
| OTHER COSTS | £ ..................... |

## TODAY'S HIGHLIGHTS

.........................................
.........................................
.........................................
.........................................
.........................................
.........................................
.........................................

## TO DO TOMORROW

...............................................................
...............................................................
...............................................................
...............................................................

# NOTES

........................................................................................

........................................................................................

........................................................................................

........................................................................................

........................................................................................

........................................................................................

........................................................................................

........................................................................................

# SKETCH / KEEPSAKE / PHOTOGRAPH

# MOTORHOME
# TRAVEL JOURNAL

DATE ...................... MILEAGE START ........................

START TIME ............... MILEAGE END ........................

ARRIVAL TIME ............... MILEAGE TOTAL ........................

---

CAMPSITE NAME ........................................

ADDRESS 1 ........................................

ADDRESS 2 ........................................

POST CODE ..................... GPS ........................

E MAIL ........................ PHONE ........................

WEBSITE WWW ........................................

MY RATING ☆ ☆ ☆ ☆ ☆ NUMBER OF NIGHTS HERE ......

WEATHER ........................ TEMPERATURE ........................

---

## WILDCAMPING LOCATION NOTES

........................................
........................................
........................................
........................................
........................... GPS ........................

| DAILY COSTS | TODAY'S HIGHLIGHTS |
|---|---|
| SITE FEES £ ..................... | ........................ |
| FUEL £ ..................... | ........................ |
| PROPANE £ ..................... | ........................ |
| TOLLS £ ..................... | ........................ |
| GROCERIES £ ..................... | ........................ |
| DINING OUT £ ..................... | ........................ |
| ENTERTAINMENT £ ..................... | ........................ |
| OTHER COSTS £ ..................... | ........................ |

## TO DO TOMORROW

........................................
........................................
........................................
........................................

# NOTES

......................................................................................................

......................................................................................................

......................................................................................................

......................................................................................................

......................................................................................................

......................................................................................................

......................................................................................................

## SKETCH / KEEPSAKE / PHOTOGRAPH

# MOTORHOME
# TRAVEL JOURNAL

DATE ..................... MILEAGE START .........................

START TIME ............... MILEAGE END .........................

ARRIVAL TIME ............... MILEAGE TOTAL .........................

CAMPSITE NAME ............................................

ADDRESS 1 ............................................

ADDRESS 2 ............................................

POST CODE ..................... GPS ..............................

E MAIL ........................ PHONE ..............................

WEBSITE WWW ............................................

MY RATING ☆ ☆ ☆ ☆ ☆ NUMBER OF NIGHTS HERE ......

WEATHER ......................... TEMPERATURE .....................

## WILDCAMPING LOCATION NOTES

............................................
............................................
............................................
............................................
.......................... GPS .....................

## DAILY COSTS

SITE FEES £ .....................

FUEL £ .....................

PROPANE £ .....................

TOLLS £ .....................

GROCERIES £ .....................

DINING OUT £ .....................

ENTERTAINMENT £ .....................

OTHER COSTS £ .....................

## TODAY'S HIGHLIGHTS

............................................
............................................
............................................
............................................
............................................
............................................
............................................

## TO DO TOMORROW

............................................

............................................

............................................

............................................

# NOTES

......................................................................................

......................................................................................

......................................................................................

......................................................................................

......................................................................................

......................................................................................

......................................................................................

......................................................................................

# SKETCH / KEEPSAKE / PHOTOGRAPH

# MOTORHOME
# TRAVEL JOURNAL

DATE .................... MILEAGE START .......................

START TIME ............... MILEAGE END .......................

ARRIVAL TIME .............. MILEAGE TOTAL .......................

---

CAMPSITE NAME .............................................

ADDRESS 1 .................................................

ADDRESS 2 .................................................

POST CODE .................... GPS .........................

E MAIL ......................... PHONE .....................

WEBSITE WWW ...............................................

MY RATING ☆ ☆ ☆ ☆ ☆ NUMBER OF NIGHTS HERE ......

WEATHER ......................... TEMPERATURE .............

---

## WILDCAMPING LOCATION NOTES

.................................................................

.................................................................

.................................................................

.................................................................

.......................................... GPS ..................

---

| DAILY COSTS | | TODAY'S HIGHLIGHTS |
|---|---|---|
| SITE FEES | £ ............... | ........................... |
| FUEL | £ ............... | ........................... |
| PROPANE | £ ............... | ........................... |
| TOLLS | £ ............... | ........................... |
| GROCERIES | £ ............... | ........................... |
| DINING OUT | £ ............... | ........................... |
| ENTERTAINMENT | £ ............... | ........................... |
| OTHER COSTS | £ ............... | ........................... |

## TO DO TOMORROW

.................................................................

.................................................................

.................................................................

.................................................................

# NOTES

............................................................................................

............................................................................................

............................................................................................

............................................................................................

............................................................................................

............................................................................................

............................................................................................

## SKETCH / KEEPSAKE / PHOTOGRAPH

Printed in Great Britain
by Amazon